# Spring Flowers

Katie Peters

GRL Consultants,
Diane Craig and Monica Marx,
Certified Literacy Specialists

Lerner Publications ◆ Minneapolis

**Note from a GRL Consultant**
This Pull Ahead leveled book has been carefully designed for beginning readers. A team of guided reading literacy experts has reviewed and leveled the book to ensure readers pull ahead and experience success.

Lerner Publications Company
A division of Lerner Publishing Group, Inc.
241 First Avenue North
Minneapolis, MN 55401 USA

For reading levels and more information, look up this title at www.lernerbooks.com.

Main body text set in Memphis Pro 24/39
Typeface provided by Linotype.

Photo Acknowledgments
The images in this book are used with the permission of: © Shutterstock, pp. 3, 4–5, 6–7, 8–9, 10–11, 12–13, 14–15, 16 (top left), 16 (top center), 16 (top right), 16 (bottom left), 16 (bottom center), 16 (bottom right)

Front cover: © Shutterstock

**Library of Congress Cataloging-in-Publication Data**

Names: Peters, Katie, author.
Title: Spring flowers / Katie Peters.
Description: Minneapolis, MN : Lerner Publications, [2020] | Series: Seasons all around me (Pull ahead readers - Nonfiction) | Audience: Ages 4–7. | Audience: K to grade 3. | Includes index.
Identifiers: LCCN 2018058182 (print) | LCCN 2018060788 (ebook) | ISBN 9781541562363 (eb pdf) | ISBN 9781541558700 (lb : alk. paper) | ISBN 9781541573451 (pb : alk. paper)
Subjects: LCSH: Flowers—Juvenile literature. | Spring—Juvenile literature.
Classification: LCC SB406.5 (ebook) | LCC SB406.5 .P48 2020 (print) | DDC 508.2—dc23

LC record available at https://lccn.loc.gov/2018058182

Manufactured in the United States of America
1 – CG – 7/15/19

# Contents

# Spring
# Flowers

In the spring,

it gets warm outside.

The snow melts.

Flowers start to grow.

I see them everywhere.

Flowers grow on trees.
There are white flowers on
this apple tree.

Flowers grow on bushes.

I see pink flowers on

this bush.

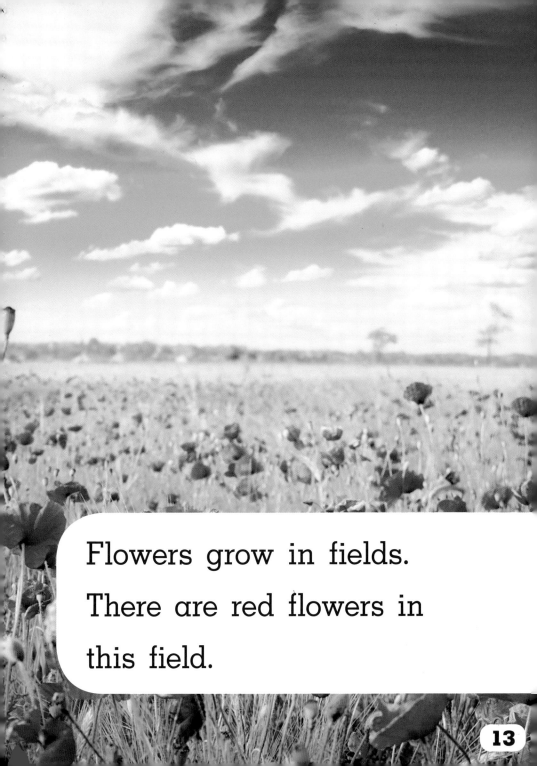

Flowers grow in fields.
There are red flowers in
this field.

Flowers grow in my garden.

I like spring flowers.

# Did You See It?

bush

field

flowers

garden

snow

tree

# Index